The Poetry Modern

Leslie H Hanna

chipmunkapublishing
the mental health publisher

Published by
Chipmunkapublishing
United Kingdom

http://www.chipmunkapublishing.com

ISBN   978-1-78382-105-1

Chipmunkapublishing gratefully acknowledge the support of Arts Council England.

My Fenian Body

My misshapen body
Fenian body
The eunuch body
I sucked a pig's penis
Pig spunk
The fuck beauty of Ruth
Youth of the flower
My devotion to truth
Perversion of mind and body
I am the papist of the fields
Rape the fenian girl
In her beauty and body
The god fuck
She is the Pearl of the mass
The flower girl
I am female of body
My failure of boy
The bull charge
I painted with the girls
Joy of nude the model
She is a modern god
The fenian Art School
Idiot beast of fool
I run across the fields, nude
Dance among wild flowers
With Moya Docherty
I gave her a child
We were wed fenian
The idiot fenian painter
I love her body
Perfect in the pig's eyes
The eyes of Moya
I am the body of man
The god fuck
I made love to the fenian
The fuck scene
Structure of life
Wife and drunk of poem
Spit in the face
Painter of the place
In field of wild flowers

Mass of Buttercups

Beast dandelion daisy field
Raise land of flowers
The beauty weed wilderness
Long live dandelion
In the land of wild flower
Sand, beach and sea
The peach tree
Of a foreign earth
The child of Berthe
Drunk of flower
Woman of Ireland
The daisy land
God is a wilderness
The modern dandelion
The god field
In the morning
I am England born
I am dead of flower
Homestead of goat
She is mother flower
The other way
Day of Henry
The poem in the summer
Poem into wild flowers
I love wild flower
The child of the daises
Beauty summer flower
The god buttercup
Fag butt in the dead ground
The magic drag of opium
Summer poppy beauty
The slop pig food
Bread and water
Sty summer field
Feed the pig of England
Breed the sow
Mother England buttercups
Beauty mass of yellow
Below hellin paint daisy
The god bluebell
The opium summer
Burn stuff in beauty land

The Lesbian Painter

Lesbian is dead pussy
The woman beauty
She is hell paint poetry
Hanna love painted female
Hate man flowers
I masturbate over the love
Above the beauty
Laugh at me in hell
Paint the body
God lesbian hell
The modern painted love
Woman to woman
Burn the flowers
Purpose of man and woman
Poem painted orgasm
The lesbian painter
The love penis
Beautiful scene of fuck
Lesbian spasm of flowers
Orgasm of female
Failure in the chair
The pale flesh
Woman of Japan
Beautiful soft muscle
Pussy of poem flower
I love Yoko Ono
I am man of flower
I love flowers of hell
The smelling fuck love bed
The dead fuck
I am the paint of poem
Face of lesbian eunuch
A place of hell
She is lady of Spain
Sadie loves Gretta
I am body of insane
The fuck distortion
Abortion of the child
The fuck wild
Buck idiot of Spain
The insane penis
Mad lesbian fuck

Pearl

God hedge winter leafless
Flowers in the wilderness
I saw god and fire
Barbed wire
Pearl is nude
Little girl of the daisy
God raise leaf and flower
Into poetry of love bluebell
The prison cell
Pearl is ghost of dandelion
Perversion of flowers
Pearl is 250 year
Beer of Ireland
I am beast hell and fire
Barbed wire of god
Fuck female angel
Dandelion and bluebell
Pearl of England
The daisy girl dandelion
Beast dandy flower
The sunny morn
Beast is the fat boy
Joy and cat
The overcoat and hat
I am the goat
In field of happiness
The damp wilderness
After rain in joy insane
No wind is god
This is my beauty
I love wild flower
The child drunk and hat
Fat boy is joy fuck
Huck Flynn of Ireland
The god dandelion
Daisy chains and dance
In beauty Pearl
The little girl of Ireland
Perversion of flowers
The loving fuck wild
The child death of England

The Stampede

My distortion of body
God waist and leg
The bust of Henry
Withered and winter flower
Abortion of woman and god
The modern poem
Female hips of Henry
The failure of the chair
Chair of fate
There among the daisies
Masturbate flower of god
Henry the eunuch
Poems of the eunuch
Suck stem fuck Rachel
In the daisy land
Stand over England's field
The fuck dance
Entrance paint of England
The Daffodils
The great poem
Poem of the still born
I am morning flower
Beast of poem
Where is flower
The flower homeland
England the fields
Born McGinty's goat
A fenian Ireland
The protestant land
McGinty drunk idiot
This is Ireland
There is no beauty
The dead flowers
Summer stunted tree
Honeybees and buttercups
Daisy flower is my beauty
My dead eye Henry
Dandelion of Ireland
Stand in field of mad
Stampede bullocks of Ireland
Penis of Ireland

Easter 1971

Dandelion poetic speech
The summer of peach
Of dream flower beast
The Easter of dandelion
I walk in the sun
Of flowers and poetry
The summer is done beauty
Of daisy buttercup poem
Lie down among flowers
A cuckoo singing
England is dandelion
Book of Kells
Painted in Ireland
Saint of the fenians
Early flower of monk
Stunk piss of sty
Eye of the pig
I lie nude in shite
Sunlight big boy dandelion
The flower horizion
Poppy rise of opium summer
The painted gum of beast
Easter 1971 is beauty
Memory of the pond
Reflections on the water
Daughter of England daisy
The fish jump
Jumbo boy of poem
I stand in awe of beauty
This the beauty of summer
Nudity and swim
Of the dream naturism
I am dandelion of weed flower
Vandemons land
I stand of poetry
In the flower of day
I will die the way of flower
Lie in the water
Penis erect and poem
The expectant daughter

The Beauty

Life poem of flower
Bluebell god poem
Wife heaven and hell
I am an idiot
Lie among flowers and trees
Speak to god
I cross myself
Sing of flower and modern hell
England the dream of poem
Paint The Scream
The day of the flower
Saint of Ireland
Flower in my hand
I am the drunk in the fields
I cross myself
I love the fenian woman
Of the bluebell
I love my god and poem
I saw the nude priest
Speech and the flower in hell
Preach of god and bluebell
The drunken idiot
Riot of the ghosts
England victory in hell
I sing among the flowers
The magic flower of bluebell
Stage of the idiot
Idiot of society of flowers
The deity of fenian
The republican stronghold
Bold fenian flower
I love the fenian god
Idiot of the modern world
The mad beast
I am Easter drunken flower
Of god and bluebell
Hell and dead land
Hand on her thigh
Hands on young woman
Lie among flower
I was the beautiful guy
Idiot and fall of beauty

Boy of Female Beauty

Lovers of beauty
The god and the bluebell
Flowers I love
The hell god and flower
I see flower of nude
I am the woodlander
Hand on body of Deidre
The god presence of idiot
Beauty of the female
The chain of failure
Flowers everywhere
I have the female beauty
Idiot of fuck
Riot on the street
Buck goat and buttermilk
Summer of the wheat land
I love dandelion
Dandelion of my god
Modern art of sunflowers
The charge of the bull
Stomach full of beer and bread
Homestead of the deer
The home of poem Ireland
The idiot of perversion
Love of god
I spunk over the chair
Flower of Deidre everywhere
Suck her breast
Hand sunk between her legs
Drunken dandelion
Hegarty idiot of Ireland
The indulgence in idiot fuck
I masturbate in summer
Fate of our lust
Hand on her bust
The dandelion of Dee
We did not buck the penis
Beauty of a fenian body
My hand on her thigh
Lie down buck Ireland poem

The Beaut Honey

The pearl heaven white stone
Early morning sunlight
Born of summer sun
The swan moan
Haven of summer swan
Daisy in hell
I love bluebell morning
The beauty of flower
The pearl heaven
In summer sun
The flower of hun
I love Emily painted beauty
Saint of the flower
In hand the blue tulip
Love the flower
Of heaven morn and summer
The idiot of England
Drunk of the flowers
In the autumn beast
Flowers die winter field
I lie among dead tulip
The drip of dew
Sap of the stem flower
Suck the blue flower poem
Flower rosy hue god
Honey spoon god
Moor of the daisy buttercup
I love dandelion
The flower of the beast
The fenian McCartan
My fenian descent
The scent of flowers
Bean is beauty nude
I love Gertrude
She is the flower love
I masturbate the flower
Flower and love
Paint and poem honey
The sunny land of flowers
Heaven the beautiful honey
Poem of the beautiful
The beautiful flower

The Sunny Land

Insanity of the mind
The dead sun
Begun of the wild flower
Dandelion of a child
I love yellow flower of the sun
Summer flower and buttercup
I utter poetry of summer flowers
The sunny land of Ireland
The dove summer flower
I am mad of the flowers
Day by day beauty chair
In the sunny land daisy
Beautiful wild flower
Dandelion is god
The tulip modern summer
Poem the beauty bluebell
I dream the prison cell
The place of my own
A bed and chair
The flower head and paint
There with pencil of my hell
Pencil is hell is poem
I paint on the wall
Poem fall of the empire
The London cell
I fell in love with Bean
Fenian of England
The dandelion love
Singing The Soldier's Song
The uniform of hell
Love the cell
The England of my birth
The poems of a eunuch
Berthe is beauty
Of fuck dandelion
I am Spud of 1916
Mud fight and bullocks
The Dublin sunlight of morn
Lyn is beauty flower
God is dandelion
I greet you in coat and hat
I am the fat boy baby face

Angel

The dandelion flower
Yellow prophecy
The poetry of hell
Smelling beast poem flower
Stem of my heart of mother
The hallucination of carthorse
I saw the bull
My full gut of beer
The locked cell
Shut behind bars
Poems in the cell
I saw the world
In solitude
Nude on the bed
Bread and water
London daughter of fire
The desire and woman
The god wine
Beer of England drunk
The year of flower
Dandelion people of god
I am born again in poem
Morning of flowers
On my knees I pray to god
Recite poem
Love of god
The poem to god of daisy
Before my eyes
Whore of Ireland
God peace and cell
Yelling of the flower
The drunk evangelist
Angel of god
I pissed the bed
The beautiful bread
The flower beauty
Cold water in hell
I kissed female angel
I see pale moon
The syrup spoon
Buttercups weed of beauty
The fuck angel
Cell is dead

Poem of Poem

The fear of dust and rustic beer
A poetic love of buttercup
Utter the poem ecstasy
Poem into prophecy
Flowers of poem
The love of flower
I am drunk with the beautiful
She is flower Janine
The god fenian beauty
Dust is cocaine
The smoke insane
Murder the flower
The powder of heaven
Addiction of Jennifer
Jennifer Jupiter
The month of june
Dust is fag of beauty
Fag of the dead land
Smoke the sunrise
Of dreamer of chair
Under the chair
She pissed herself
Virgin on the shelf
Urge of flower love
Is fenian flower of god
The wench modern art
The park bench
God beach and the nudes
Preach the god of woman
Poem modern
Lichen and fern
Man in god's likeness
I confess my sins
Repent of Hanna
The Hanna lament in the garden
The beer and painting
Saint drunk Spike
Spike the drunk beast
The sunken garden
The ferment yeast bread
The dandelion bread
Hanna of Ireland
The poems of Hanna

The Hat

Tom cat is mad
Sat on the bull
Full of England beer
The hat on his shaved head
The dead man bullock
The ginger Tom
Mock the Union Jack
A pin the cat's back
Insane house of madness
Dressed in uniform
The man of Glengormley
Henry and the bullock generation
I stampede the field
Of dandelion flower
Hour of dieing
I will die painted flower
Tom Saint Cat
I am the bull of Ireland
The bullock field of madness
Dressed in green, white and gold
An old man's penis
The senile generation
Smile cat of England
Pinstripe style suit
Recruit the mad
I am the bad boy of the asylum
The summer joy
Coming of the fucker
The Downshire mucker
I love blondie of Ireland
Of Viking descent
Scent of flowers
Spike in the field
Luscious mushrooms of Henry
Doom in the London room
The chair of poetry
I went to the psychiatrist
Clench in the fist
A dig in the guts
The cut eye
Die in the field of flowers
The hours with blondie

Poem The Beauty

My god in the fields and the flowers
Oh heaven beauty
God descended around me
In buttercup and daisy
My poem daisy
Praise my god of wilderness
The drunkenness and fag
I shag a maiden
Among flower and tree
The honey bee
The cuckoo sound
Beauty wild flower
The buttercup of fag
That sweet smoke
Flowers of my god
I am in the fields of Ireland
Yield of poppies
The dandelion smoke
Poppy of opium dreamers
The summer of flowers
I love Mona of Ireland
My land is dandelion
Dandelion is England
The beauty sun
I painted flowers of god
In the meadow of sun
The beauty summer
The beauty Mona of Ireland
I paint her nude
Poem of woodland nature
I am the sunrise
The sunflowers of Ireland
Beauty morn love surprise
The Easter Rising
Death of an Irish beast
Ireland the beast
I am a dieing flower
God's dower of beauty
Beauty is dieing
I see the flowers of beauty
I poem field
Poem is my beauty
This is my love of god

Swan of England

The painted swan
Sawn of her beauty
Poem cello of England
Dance in hell
Enhance the swan
Dance the swans of England
Emotion of a boy
Sleeping Beauty the cry of youth
Die in a field
Who is Ruth
Paint and the cello
Obsession of a piano
The Hanna painted flower
Saint of the field
The yield of corn
Summer morning the flower
Henry is dead
In the bed of his room
Doom of the flowers
Swan of a lake and cello
Mother paint swan
Saint Cecilia of England
England is the swan
The nostalgia of my youth
Paint in Ireland
Ruth is beautiful
A dull day in England of the swan
I watch over stunted life
England is the midwife
Born in beauty
Of flower and cello
Morn painted swan
Gone to hell
God is bluebell
God among flowers of field
I love my god
Paint below hell
Poem above Eden
The morning is yellow
I am the fellow of beauty
Lie down above flower

Man in the Mountain

Garden Narcissus
The flower Gus
Gardener Gus Ireland flower
Tulips of Amsterdam
Gus is goat and ram
God in the mountain and dam
I saw god garden of mountain
Gus grew the flowers
They beauty of garden
In the wild
Woman and child
Wilderness of goat
Milk of goat and drunkenness
The raw milk
And home brew
I grew vegetables
The spit of the wild deer
Beer and good food
I am beast of love of flower
Above meadow tulips
She is Mildred home bread
My woman and son
Wild of mountain
Fountain of poem
Poems of Gus and bluebell
The garden poem
Angel of hell
The drunk camp fire
Damp after rain no wind
This is my joy
A full day is my beauty
Full of beer and venison
The garden in the wilderness
Dressed in deer skin
We are dandelion
Beast of the flower
The dower god and buttercup
I utter the flower after the storm
I stand nude in rain
I am insane beast
The storm is my beauty
My woman is beauty
Dry in summer sun
Morning is done

The Ditch

The god land of flower
Scene of beauty
Flower of god
God descend the Art Modern
House and court of old Ireland
Paint and poem lemon god
In autumn beauty
The summer flowers
Study flower, the hair of beauty
My garden chair
Paint light on the stair
Window yellow light
Meadow beyond the garden
Fade light winter day
Shade and white flower
The beauty autumn
God above wild flower
The child in the meadow
The day of god
Beyond the flower beauty
I see the white house
The garden of truth
Flowers of my youth
Drink and poem flower
Poem of spunk and beer
A year in Ireland
Poem in Ireland
The flowers of Ireland
The made people spunk
Drunken people of flower
God indulgence in the world
Sentence to the cell
Poems of the cell
I was the gardener
Pitch fork and ditch
Pitch of Ireland
The lovers in a bed of leaves
Pitch fork of Ireland
In the gut
Die spunk and drunk
Poem of Ireland dandelion

Kitsch

In green field the flower grow
Flower scene in a row
Of dandelion and burdock
In the pint jar
Old days of flower
Bold Wigan and poem
Nostalgia and dereliction
I am the boy of the field
The slag heap
The fag deep smoke
Hanna home Wigan
My birth homeland
Old England of mother
The bull ring
Sinclair Place the house of Hanna
The mines of Wigan
Hub of the north land
I grow the flowers
The dead land stunt growth
The smoke and fume
Prophecy on Wigan pier
Poetry of beer
Mother of Wigan in her beauty
The Woodbine fag
Drag of flower smoke
The Hippodrome
Home and wild flowers
Wedding of mother
Father in pinstripe
The love birds
Words of poem in Ireland
The field of beauty
The Ireland field
Fenian descent
Descent of England Jew
The beautiful field
Remains of the land of flower
I am insane poem field
The Wigan Jew
Ireland home brew
A drunken poem of England
Drunk of Ireland
The drunk in kitchen chair

The Cello

Beauty swan the cello
I made love to the swan
The love hell
Yellow light of sun
Love the cello
Music beast beauty
Of the flowers
Shower in sunlight
The god dower
The Dvorziak Humoresque
Concerto of swan
Fresco in Florence
Painted swan of engalnd
Sentence in poem
The beast love-flower
Cello in hell
I made love to the cello
The body of woman
The swan fuck
Beauty of cello
Among flower on a sunny day
Of honey and humming bee
The summer day
Mona plays cello
In eth heaven studio
Angels surround
Sound of Dvorzak
In beauty cello
Meadow of god the white house
Light of the sun
The shadow flowers
Madness of swan
Love in hell
The beauty of fuck
She is swan
Passion of the cello
Fuck and female
I love music beautiful
Mad of the beautiful
In heaven of light
Midnight of cello

Morn of the summer

The bust of the flowers
Poetic lust of beauty
Hours of love
In the room alone
Flower of Pearl
In early light of summer morn
Rite of Spring
The fuck and music
Poetic and pedantic maiden
The faded flower
The sour buttermilk
Flutter the dance
Butterfly
We stand nude
In the morning light
The white flowers
Ireland the flowers of daisy
We lay in morning dew
Fuck and song bird
Ireland the thrush
The singing sparrow
Bud the flowers of the hedgerow
The edge of the world
Songbird and flowers
Poem of the summer sunlight
If white flower
Pearl the beauty
The nudity and flowers
I love the flowers
My madness of flower
Poetry of flower wild
A child was born
In the nudity of the flowers
A boy of Ireland
Pearl the mother of my child
In early morn
Born of the flowers
I am Hanna of paint nude
Feud of Ireland beauty
Saint of Pearl
Pearl of Ireland
The flower girl maiden
Flowers of my madness
Fuck among singing bird

She is Deidre

Painter of the flower
I greet you in this hour
Of a madness
Sadness of a flower
I am flower poem
The god lemon
God in a lemon tree
The England sea
Speak to me my god
I saw you among the flowers
Flower god wild bluebell
The flower spell
U greet the friends of England
I was there
The Daffodils of Wordsworth
Berthe of stick flower
Painted in stillness
Drunkenness and flowers
I lay me down among them
Flower ruby gem
England the stem
The love of Ireland
The dead land
Of the potato famine
Easter Rising 1916
The beast of the scene
The final inferno
This is the dieing
Beautiful hereafter
Returns to the wilderness
This is god's land
This sit eh flower
Moments of beauty
An irishman's indulgence
Paint the wilderness
Of Gaeltacht pitch fork
Irish girl from Cork
Lust with the Pearl of Ireland
We did not fuck
Hands on her body beautiful body

Whiskey Sunday

England the flower
The hour of the beast
A sour lemon of god
God of lemon tree
Three crosses on Golgotha
Moss of tree
 A white horse purgatory
The fat woman
I am John Cat of England
Sin of the flowers
Hours of drunk
Ireland – America of skunk
I am of England born
The life of Ireland
Whiskey of Sunday
Drunk of morn
Ireland of my father
The Ulster scot
Grandfather of Ireland
Pitchfork and gun
The sun of flowers
I am Protestant Ireland
Hate of the Fenian
Fate of the scene
God save the queen
I am England of mother
Flowers of another god
I stood on Wigan pier
Briefcase and prophecy
Poetry of Ireland
Here in Wigan
A business man in pinstripe suit
Snipe shooting in England
The shotgun wedding
Flower of England is done
I am dead man of Ireland
We are dandelion men
Men of Henry
This is the dead land
Spud of Ireland
I am Henry spud
The bud flower of spring

The morn

I in my madness
Write the poem of mad
Flower summer mad
The sad Ruth
In yield of youth and poem
Lemon of china
Sermon beast flowers
Beer of god
Year 1811 heaven buttercups
Flutter butterfly
Dance the butterfly
Of dry flower
In a meadow and sunlight
The honeysuckle flower
Bee suckle the flower
Of Ireland honey
The beautiful flower
Of the yellow stem
Poem into beauty
Dandelion beautiful
And daisy
Meadow flower shadow and light
Midnight and daisy
Raise the swan
Into oblivion
Lemon of poem
In the godland
The poem modern
I yearn for flowers of summer
The wild fern of woodland
Nude of naturism
Futurism of poetry
Future of the dam
Goat and ram
I am born of yellow moon
Cello of Ruth
Solo on heaven
Eleven angels
The poeticism and music
The lemon flower
God and summer Ireland
Poem in summer
The morning is yellow

Gothic Beauty

Swan the beauty female flower
Slender of white
Swan over Ireland
Flight and dead land
Beauty female over mad
Mad men of mental house
In the garden of men and women
Men see beauty
The promiscuity and flowers
The love flowers
Old Ireland modern god
I am the fat boy
The hat and the flowers
Cat killed the pig
Die Lyndsey in the sky
Song of Lyndsey
The pink eyes
Mena and the fag
Hag of Ireland fat woman
Hat of Ireland
Swan is female beauty
Gothic maiden swan
The poetic Pearl
Little ghosty girl of Ireland
Pearls and flowers
200 years old in her madness
Maiden swan is Judith
A gothic nude
Brothel of Ireland
The truth of bothie
Youth in mental house
A scented flower of blue
Dew of Judith flower
Japan the flower
The ice-cream man
Dream in madness in Ireland
A painted hell the cellar of whiskey and beer
A year of madness
Pearl is the swan
Siobhan is the lesbian
Gothic beauty of woman

Ireland Sun

Castrate the flower
Sinew of gut
Dew the summer morn
Born in the hut
Of poem and prophecy
The midnight moon
Blue hut among trees
Day of summer
The honey bees
The flower morn
God dower of sunlight
Midnight heaven spoon
Of honeysuckle
Bullock field and muck
Suckle the flowers
The hum of the bees
Apple tree garden
Flowers and vegetables
Ireland of pitch fork
Smoke the cork
Fag of Ireland paint flower
Boy of the flowers
Painter of chain and light
Chair and flowers
Hours of summer day
The way through flowers
To the place I love
The bank of the dam
Dragonfly and poem
Dance the butterfly
The utterance
Beer cans and flower
The year 2010
The Yellow Men
Men of spud head
The cud of bullock
I am gut full beer
Poem in Ireland
The summer day
I lay me down
In green pastures
The scene of Ireland sun

Philosophy of Flower

Poetry of flowers
Philosophy of flower
In the beauty of light
Exuberance of flowers
Love of the beauty
In the beautiful land
Stand in god's light
Of beautiful flowers
I love the flower
Heaven dove and the daisy
Simple wild flower
A child and daisy chains
Flower of god the sane
I am the gardener of wild
Pain of the flower
Born of woman
Return to the primitive
Flower of man
Of born and pitchfork
The flowers of Ireland
The lust maiden of Cork
Fade bust of Deidre
Kiss her breast
Hands up her thigh
Hands on female body
The green garden gate
Fate of fuck
I dream the fuck of Ireland
Under laburnum tree
The girl flower
Poetry of flower
The philosophy of light
Rite of Spring
The beginning and god
Poem modern is flower
Lemon of modern
Philosophy of the human values
Female of flower
The pale sunlight
God and beast in hell
Second coming yellow flower

The Fields

Beast of the dam
Stripped to the waist
Goat and ram
Eunuch in the sunshine
The final moment
Scent of flowers in summer
Ripped shirt of a boy
Joy lake young girl
Pearl and the flowers
Sun and showers
The wild flowers of Ireland
Retreat to the field
Yield of wheat and rye
Die the flower
A deformed body
Mind and gut
Smoke the fag butt
Boy trip into smoke
The tulip god
Beauty of Amsterdam
The ram in England
Henry the eunuch
Fuck pearl early sun
Eunuch fuck beauty
Moon of female
The pale sun
The honeysuckle
Bee suckle flower
In beautiful land
Of the white goat
Coat of multi colour
The dreamer's coat
A drunken boy in Ireland
School uniform burn flower
Burn the uniform
In hell modern history
Story of Henry Hanna
I am Seamus of flowers
Poet of Ireland
The white horse in hell
I am drunk of the fields

Wheatland

The dandelion flower
Weed of the beast
Dandelion water is beauty flower
Ireland is the flower of seed
I am the sower
Painted of the fields
God of the field
Painted dandelion madness
Ruth paint sadness of weed
Fuck among dandelion
The beauty god
Of modern flower England
I stand in Wigan field
Stunted tree of god
Humming bee honeysuckle
Home honey flower
The honey sweet beauty
The wheatland beast
Easter Monday 1971 the god
Of flower opium
Poem beauty of godland
Beast of honey field
The flower yield
God love flower mad
I am flower madness
The mess of flower prophecy
Smoke the opium flower
Broken light of god
I am best honey
I am the flowers
Seek ye the god
Of the wheatland
Harvest autumn sun
The beautiful land
Beast is the beautiful land
In paint and without light
Field without darkness
My madness is flower
In light of morn
I see without light
I heard a cuckoo sing
England the wheatland

Poems of My Home

Flowers of England are dead
The beauty lives
The god and England
I am modern art
Poem in London
Semi-nude Judy
She is maiden of hell
Hand up her thigh
Old man of lust
The park bench old Henry
Sober old man
Painter of a child
Saint wild flower
Speak of poetry
Recite La Figlia Che Piange
Sunlight on the stair
Dieing in the chair
Dummy in the chair of hell
The dandelion people
England the dandelion
The sunlight garden
Weave the strands of thread
A dead beast of England
My England
The England mother
Another kind of joy
A boy in heaven
Drunk of old Ireland
Paint and England poem
Paint old Ireland mad
Summer of Hanna poetry
Seamus Hanna fenian
My poems in England
Of Ireland dandelion
I stand in Ireland
Poem id Mozart Amadeus
Amadeus genius in hell
A fenian cellist
The cello in hell
I am Hanna concerto
Perversion of music boy

Immortal Plough

Fade the flower
The maiden of England
Of wild dandelion
Wild flower beauty of the field
The child is mad
Sun and bullock field
Stampede and yellow dandelion
Weed of England flower
Beast fuck and summer
Immortal plough of Ireland
Sow in god's ground
Pig sty of wasteland
I dug fenian ground
Flowers of a protestant land
Pregnant maiden in England
To hell for eternity
Paint finite woman
Colour without light
The sight of England
Aphrodite goddess of love
Face flower of madness
Die immortal plough
Lie in the sty of sow
Cry the beauty of Ireland
Dandelion of my speech
I preach people of the plough
England born again
The beast bull insane
The full gut beer
Speech of god is here
In Ireland now
The Ireland of the sow
Born in England of England mother
Father of Ireland drunk
I am the dandelion born
In the sun of bullock field
Morning of England
The wheat yield
I preach to the mad people
Ireland sadness of bull
The beer of the gut drunkenness

1971

A drunken penis in the bar
Piss in the pants
The big pint jar
Young woman kiss, pints of beer
The year 1971
I wet myself in sunlight
Pure white milk of the goat
Thick raw milk
The stink of piss
Beer milk honeywater
In sunny England
Of dandy flower
Silk shirt and pants
The beer piss
Alcohol of the gut
Warhol and cut fag
Painter of the Marilyn Monroe
The sloe gin
The drunken Irishman
A virgin soldier
Fuck the virgin wench
The boy and the workbench
The Apprentice Boys
Of Derry protestant
Fenian Derry busted gut
Mustard tomato sandwich
The witch of England
I am the fat boy
Apprentice sheet metal worker
The wheatland
Wheat field and dandelion
I am the dandelion field
The wheat yield
I am bust gut descent
Scent of fenian flower
Ireland bent god
The bent flower stem
Of poem England
Flower stand in hell
The beer and buck steer
In the wild of Ireland
A child rides the goat

Poem of a Child

Youth and cat shit
The stink was awful
Fat boy Ireland
Pink Floyd and all that Jazz
I sat in the chair and dandelions
Arazmataz Chelsea girls
Spike loves Pearl
Spike in hell
Yellow flower cornfield
Bull and dandelion
Roam the fields of wheat and rye
Die beauty dream
Scream the flowers
I watch with awe
Hour by hour
The sour fruit lemon
Poem beauty suck dandelion
Dandy fag of dry flower
Into beautiful dream
A big mug of raw cream
Straw hat dream paint daisy
The daisy land
Praise absence of god
Painted scene has no god
The fenian modern
Sentence to atheism
Poem of god poeticism
The future of man
God and poem of a child
I love wild flower
Purpose of youth and god
Existentialism of youth
The poeticism of truth
Boy and woman
Pink Floyd maniac
The beast insane
God in poem and creation
Of man and universe
The verse of poem joy

The idiot

Thin idiot drunk
The Ireland fag
Drag of yellow smoke
Pollution of the lung
Idiot hung the pig
A shot of whiskey in the gut
Hot whiskey and the hearth
An Ireland home
The pig whiskey bog boy Lyndsey
Spit of McGinty
Side of back bacon
Idiot of McGin
Poetry of Finland
Philosophy of the new poets
A new set of dice
A slice of home bread
Of the home kitchen
I am Henry the beast
Poems of the beast
Hops yeast and barley corn
Rising sun of morn
Wake drunk and flower
Bake home made bread
The home butter
Spuds of gut Ireland
The bud berry red
I am the dead man
I am the dream of a child
Beautiful cream of the goat
The wild goat
Stoat killed the cat
Fat boy slim
The slime of the slit
Spit in the face
Chase the deer in sunlight
Prostitution of white flower
Beer of England
Ireland home flowers
Beast of flower
Flowers of my madness

The Patchway

The clearing among the trees
The pathway through
Flowers and trees either side
Tree of the yellow leaf
This is the belief in god
Beauty of the painted scene
Fenian painter of nature
Beyond is water
Pond in sunlight morn
The place I love
Born of sunlight
White and yellow flower
Fellow of nude
The way to modern flower
Yellow leaves on path of atheism
I believe in god
The poeticism and paint
Bathing pond bull rush
The weed dark water
Daughter in beautiful scene
A painted fenian eye
Die with the flowers
Summer pathway
Flower and yellow leaf
Fellow of England
Painter of England flower
I saw swan
Wild life and cuckoo sing
I weep like a child
My pathway to god
Die the flower
Sun hath shone
Elegant swan of England
A dream in my sleep
Sun steep in summer
Wild flower and nude
Born flower child
Painted in Ireland
The modern belief in beauty
I yearn for tree and flower
Sunlight hour beauty

Poem of England

Dandelion of England
The sunlight of flower
Beauty schizophrenia yellow
Spit in the face
The place of flower
Two hours in sunlight
Dull days of dandelion
Madness of a painter
Poems of a saint
Disgrace of 1970 summer
Impersonate Christ
Insult Christ of dandelion
The cult of Ireland
Ireland the fenian religion
Protestant dandelion
Field of god summer
I preach to the beast
Beast is a mass
Grass of England and dandelion
The speech of priest
Beast preach the painter
The saint of flowers
Paint the sunlight
Paint night lamp
Streets of Wigan
Cobblestones damp morn
I saw the horse and cart
Hallucination of mad
I am mad Henry Hanna
Jumbo men of Ireland
A protestant prophecy
The protestant hearth
The poem Martha
Seamus poem Dublin
Poet of Ireland the Republic
In weed of flower
Protestant is dandelion
Poems of England

Poem Henry

I am drunken Henry
Of dandelion man
Pints of beer of the dandelion
Beer on Saturday
The fat woman of beauty
Die beast of the flower
Lie down beast and die
In the fields of Ireland
Cry love of flower
God showed me a flower
The sour stem
Poem in Ireland
Stem in buttercup
I saw god among wild flower
Sunlight and beauty
In mass of buttercups
Of the grassland flower
Utterance of poem
Dance the kitchen flower
Grandma Berthe dance
Old boy drank 20 pints
The Hanna home
The church of Rome
Fenian Hanna
Sons of Berthe
A fucking laugh
My Da shipyard
Hugh barman, Robert Bass Faliery's bar
A big glass jar
Guinness of Ireland
Witness of black alcohol
Cream of Guinness
I dream the flower
A drunken state
Fate of Ireland drunk
I am the drunk
Hanna whiskey and beer
The year 2000ad
Lust with Dee

Innocence

Poem to the antichrist
Paint the second coming
My innocence of poem
40 years on love flower
The girl of England
Pearl the love
The early flowers
I am innocent of antichrist
Christ kiss Magdalene
I kiss beauty girls
I am not the Christ
I saw the third coming
Poems of "Christ Saved The World"
The lame walk, the deaf hear and the blind see
Beautiful love forever in Palestine
I am poem of the Christ
My Magdalene girls
Pearl is pre-Raphaelite
Nude in sunlight
Beauty of slender body
I painted the modern
Light on Pearl and flower
Sunlight on day
White flowers
I ran to the fields
The beauty died
Christ was crucified
I sit among wild flower
The sunlight flower
I am mad of the asylum
10 years of lunacy
The nonsense poems
I am poem of the comings
In my room of the paintings
The tomb of the Christ
I am the painter of the crucifixion
The crown of thorns
I am born in the slum
The dummy Henry Tonk
Poems of Henry
The summer fields

Die Rose in Your Heart

Mother is in my heart
Hallucinate horse and cart
The gate of Ireland
Fate of dandelion
Beer and the bar
The big glass jar
Drinking the piss
Kiss me Rose
Pose in the chair
Sunlight on the stair
Mother dance hall
Paint and party
My poem of the wall
Pink Floyd education
The beer libation
A drunk Ireland 1914
My father born
Grandfather sat drunk
The fat Hanna women
The fuck Berthe
The flower earth
Lizzy and the twins
On the bins in Ireland
Clapton is god
The experience of modern
Paint and music
Henry and art
The heart of my body
The mother heart of Hanna
Die Rose in your heart
Mother paint the weeping flower
I am poem of L.H. Hanna
The poetic Ireland
Poetry experience The Hollowmen
I recited poem from the pint
Jar in the pitch dark
And Senior Service plain
Bank of Ireland
I am drunk summer

My Youth

I am beyond the dead people
In life of Henry
I am born again
In beautiful morn
The insane painter
Of beautiful flowers
Morning is god
Pain of poetry The Hollow Men
The poetry experience
Recite on television
The white flower of dead land
The T.S. Elliot poems
Stem of my youth
The truth of desert sun
Honey flower of wild poem
The heaven honey
Spoon of god
Flower of moon
Poems of my distorted body
About penis gut
Butt of the fag
Self destruction of the beast
The bull charge
A large penis
Full of beer and the madness
The mad flower
I am a medium of the dead
Flower of dead
I love the flower
Flowers and beer
Dream of my drunkenness
The year 2020
The painting of The Scream
Bent stem of a swan
The swan is a flower
The god flower
Before my time
Juice of woman
Of man and woman

The Poetry

I paint the flower
In the studio of hell
England the wild bluebell
A child dies in his mother's arms
The charm flower
I saw mother and the asylum
Summer of the mad
Beauty of the garden
Poetry of my madness
Art school of drunk and paint
Ireland lunacy of moon
Mad man and medicine spoon
Model of nude
I saw mad house of Ireland
Memory of mother and garden home
The sad prophecy
I eat from the bowl
I see wheat field and farmstead
Immortal plough of Monaghan
The asylum of Ireland
Sow of the sty
The jaundiced eye
Stunk pig and stout
I am drunk in summer
Aunt Lizzie's gout
Lizzy whiskey hell
I remember poetry of youth
Pink Floyd experience
The sentence hell
The poetry experience
I recite poems in my drunkenness
The lemon tree
Mona of the flowers
My devotion to the truth
Poetry in my youth
I paint madness
Poems of truth and sane
Prophecies of the asylum
Dyeing summer flowers
Stink the breath of beast
The death Ireland
The fenians mad

God Stem

I am god stem
I hold god of flower
God is buttercup daisy
Poem of utterance
In field praise my god
Daisy is poem god
The modern poem
She is god stem
Blasphemy of the stem
God came to me in flower
I am forest of pale light
I am white daisy
Daisy of Ireland
I saw god among the flowers
I heard god's voice
The poeticism of word
Four boys in a public bar
Joy of beer and whiskey
Year 1916 poteen of Ireland
Grandfather Hanna the heavy drinker of Ireland
Booze and poetry
Bet on the house in England
The blues of virgin dandelion
Grass verge and buttercups
A cup of wine
A fine field of wild flowers
House of England
Win the Grand National
Sins of hell
The bells of St. Clemens
Paint the race horse
My love of flowers
A heavenly dove of peace
Soldier of the Somme
The victory of Sodom
Among wild poppies
We hung a police man
Soldier death and poppies
Lover of flower
I am god stem
The flower god in my hand

The Lemon Tree

Lemon Tree beauty Japan
The god juice
Lucy of England
I love Lucy Valentine
Shine autumn moon
The dummy in blue
Dummy lives in England
She sits in a chair of London
Plundered music dummy
In the shadow room
The doom window
I see meadow of the sun
I am the hun
Lemon tree of Japan
The lemon beast
Incest and flowers of Ireland
Ireland is lemon
Poem to Japan
Ban the paint of beast
Yeast and beer
The yeast ferment bread
Dandelion beer
Poteen Ireland potato water
Alcohol and poem
The Warhol painting
The late Marilyn Monroe
Fate of dummy in chair
My failure in chair
Dummy destruction
Suck the pig milk
Udder of buttermilk
Utterance of dance
Poem The Lemon Tree
Spring blossom flowers
Lemon tree of Japan
The poem suckle honey bee
Beauty paint summer

Homestead

Homestead of Ireland
The green white and gold
Hearth of Ireland
Home baked bread
The big brass bed
She is Sinead
Her braided long hair
In the chair of poem
God is the lemon tree of Japan
Ban the flowers of the dyeing
God the flowers
I believe in a god
A god in the dream of poem
I see god among the flowers
The painted scream of fuck
Leaves of god forest autumn
Summer of modern poem
The harvest autumn of summer
Japan the lemon god
Ireland the beauty
The painted beauty of flower
Hell is a flower bluebell
Nudity of flower
Whiskey by the hearth
The poem Hubert Hanne
The Ireland of Henry
I am Henry Hanna
The yellow man
We are the yellow of god
Yellowmen of dandelion
Poem of Ireland in paint
Exuberance of paint
Paint flowers of god
Atheism of paint
Paint has no god
Saint and tricolour Ireland
I love flowers of modern poem
The god of nature
Future of the world
Homestead and hearth
The goat of Ireland
A standing flower

Mass of Poem

Mass of the fenians
Grass and yellow flowers
The scene of the fenian mass
Cello requiem
The lemon tree
I see lemon of China
Daisy mass of yellow and white
The fenian flower
Poem of the fenian
Friends of my distorted body
God of my body the flowers
The hours of paint and poem
The lemon nude
Lemon woman fenian
I am fenian
In my gut penis and body
God the fenian god
Indulgence of paint
The fenian painter of Ireland
Poem of the indulgence
Indulgence of mass
Gold, frankincense and myrrh
The priest indulge
Passion of the Christ
Flowers of Poltergiest
Christ of the dandelion
The ghost of Christ daisy
Praise my god of flowers
Cactus of desert land
The mist and seed
The weed dandelion
Smoke the weed broken flower
Ireland wild flowers
The child and the flower
The depth of gut mass
Drunk of the gut
I am stink stunted body
Grunt glass of milk
To the head drunk clean
The mug of sweet raw milk
Dug in the stomach
Bread and butter mug of milk

The Beast

England is the angel poeticism
The poetic swan
Plasticisim of angel god
The hell flower
Modern poem in Ireland
Poetry is Ireland
The new poeticism England
Ireland the angel Patrick
Fenian angelic poem
Beast is a fenian
My love of Ireland poem
Seamus poem of swan
A goose's wing
I am singer in the rain
I am poetic insane
The neurotic beast
Ireland of flowers
Fuck among flowers
England the flower poetry
I am made of the flower
Sad beast lemon tree
The Seamus poems of Ireland
My poem is flower of Ireland
Poem of the dyeing
Swan is crying paint swan
Of poem the beast
Easter Monday 1971
Flowers in the sun
Sun shining over the land
If Ireland dry grass
The Lake dragon fly poem
A dance butterfly
The lake enhance swan
Enhancement ferment paint beast
Paint the beast
Gut and human
Fag and hut of prayer
Speech of the beast
Teacher Magee
I see a lemon tree
Humming bird
In the summer days

The Daisy Poems

The dew flower is beautiful
In full morn light
I am born in flower bluebell
And white daisy
Praise my god
In modern poem sun
Morn sun dew
They beauty stem
The dew fall light
On wild flower of a child
Of England child flower
The England wilderness
Ireland men of wild flower
The wench of England
Fuck on a bench
Dandelion of Ireland is mad
The sadness of dandelion
Eth white daisy
Praise god of sunlight fall
On modern the poetic flower
The yellow sun England morn
God is my beauty sunlight
This is beauty
The years of dead colour
The dull shade of light
Fade the dead flower
Experience death dull dandelion
The full gut of beer
The dyeing of my eyes
Cries of free Ireland
Beauty of god land
The heaven land of poem
The Protestantism of flowers
England is a flower
The fenian flower
Of Ireland is dead
The rising god of Ireland
Green white and gold
Flag of Ireland
Fag Ireland dope poem
The Ireland poem
England poem of white daisy